max science primary

Journal 6

DISCOVERING THROUGH ENQUIRY

LAWRIE RYAN

SERIES EDITOR: **BOB KIBBLE**

macmillan education

INTERNATIONAL CURRICULUM

Macmillan Education Limited
4 Crinan Street
London N1 9XW

Companies and representatives throughout the world

Journal ISBN 978-1-380-02173-1

First published 2019

Original design by EMC Design Ltd and Macmillan Education
Page make-up by Ink Design
Illustrated by Nick L'Ange, Bev Victor, Tamsin Hinrichsen, Nick L'Ange pp 2, 3, 7, 34, 39, 45, 65, 66, 70, 71, 75, 80, 85, 90; Bev Victor pp 19, 23, 30, 49, 52, 55, 56, 61, 81, 87, 91, 95, 96, 97, 98; Tamsin Hinrichsen pp 1, 12, 17, 22, 27, 33, 44, 49, 57, 60
Cover design by Sparks Publishing Services Ltd and Macmillan Education
Cover illustration by Star Publishing Pte Ltd and Jorge Santillan c/o Beehive Illustration Agency

Printed and bound in Argentina
2020
5

Contents

Introducing the *Max Science primary* Journal iv

Unit 1 Human organs and systems 1
1.1 Why do we need organs? 1
1.2 Body systems and organs 7
1.3 When organs go wrong 12

Unit 2 Reversible and irreversible changes 17
2.1 Investigating reversible and irreversible changes 17
2.2 Making and separating mixtures 22
2.3 Dissolving 27

Unit 3 Food chains 33
3.1 Living things in their habitat 33
3.2 Food chains 39
3.3 Explaining food chains 44

Unit 4 Electrical conductors and insulators 49
4.1 Circuit diagrams 49
4.2 Conductors and insulators 55
4.3 Investigating circuits 60

Unit 5 Caring for the environment 65
5.1 Spaceship Earth – the atmosphere 65
5.2 Spaceship Earth – habitats and buildings 70
5.3 Spaceship Earth – save energy and recycle 75
5.4 Spaceship Earth – taking care of my local environment 80

Unit 6 Mass and weight 85
6.1 Investigating mass and weight 85
6.2 Forces and force diagrams 90
6.3 Friction 95

Introducing the *Max Science primary* Journal

The *Max Science primary* Journal complements the *Max Science primary* series by providing a link between learning at school and learning at home. It matches the topics from the course and the Cambridge Primary Science Curriculum framework with a topic-by-topic series of structured activities for learners to complete with an adult.

As a parent or carer, it is sometimes difficult to know what is being taught in school and how your child is really doing in a subject. Do they enjoy it? Do they understand the concepts and the vocabulary? This Journal lets you spend time with your learner at home in a supportive way, to find out how they are doing in science.

Introducing the topic

A cartoon image and question introduces every science topic in a fun and engaging way.

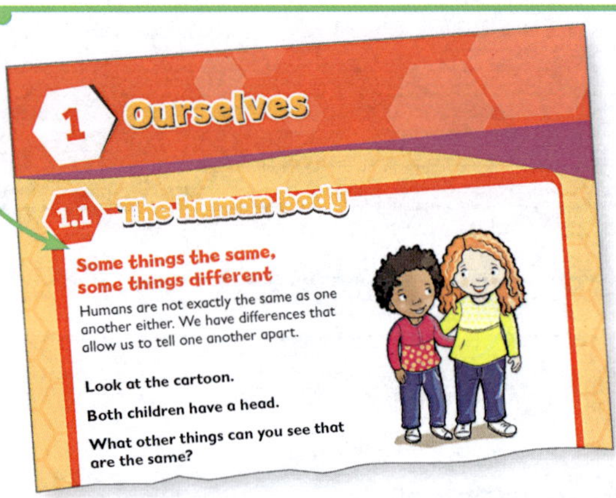
1 Ourselves

1.1 The human body

Some things the same, some things different

Humans are not exactly the same as one another either. We have differences that allow us to tell one another apart.

Look at the cartoon.

Both children have a head.

What other things can you see that are the same?

Check my science

Each topic allows learners to check their understanding through this activity.

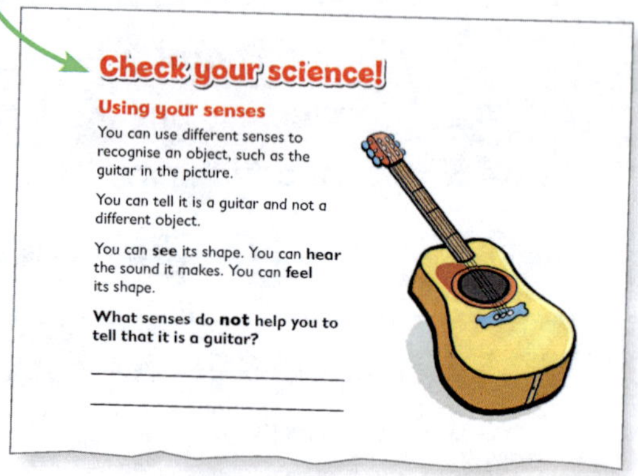
Check your science!

Using your senses

You can use different senses to recognise an object, such as the guitar in the picture.

You can tell it is a guitar and not a different object.

You can **see** its shape. You can **hear** the sound it makes. You can **feel** its shape.

What senses do not help you to tell that it is a guitar?

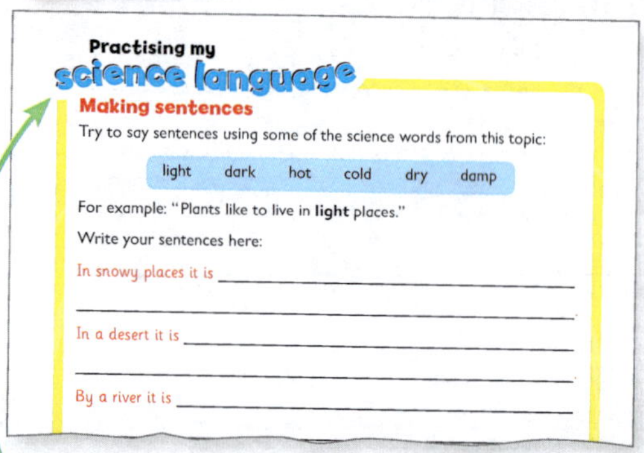
Practising my science language

Making sentences

Try to say sentences using some of the science words from this topic:

light dark hot cold dry damp

For example: "Plants like to live in **light** places."

Write your sentences here:

In snowy places it is ______

In a desert it is ______

By a river it is ______

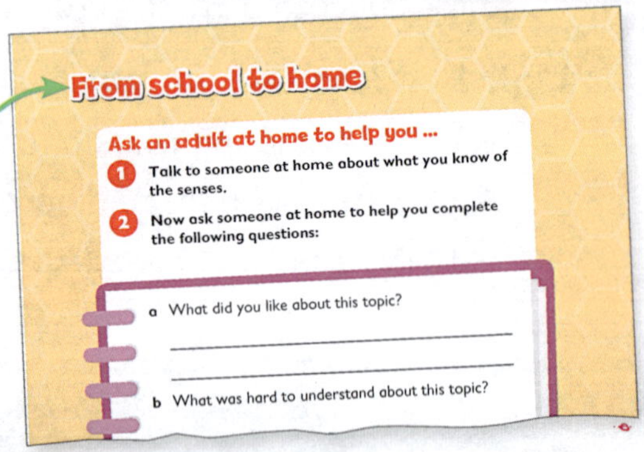
From school to home

Ask an adult at home to help you ...

1. Talk to someone at home about what you know of the senses.
2. Now ask someone at home to help you complete the following questions:

a What did you like about this topic?

b What was hard to understand about this topic?

Practising my science language

This feature provides language practice of key words to improve scientific vocabulary and to make it easier to learn science in English.

From school to home

You can work together at home to complete this section at the end of each topic. The Journal can then be taken into school for the teacher to look at and discuss, and acts as a record of the learners' progress.

1 Human organs and systems

1.1 Why do we need organs?

In this first topic in Unit 1 you should be able to identify the position of major organs in the body.

You should also be able to explain why the major organs are essential.

Sam has been learning about the organs of the body at school. His little brother asks Sam about what happens to the body when we eat at breakfast.

What should Sam tell his younger brother?

____

____

____

____

What makes Sam think that his little brother does not really know where his stomach is?

____

____

____

Check your science!

The essential processes common to all living things are:

- movement
- growth
- reproduction
- respiration
- excretion
- sensitivity
- nutrition.

1. Match each of these essential processes to one of the descriptions below:

Changing position or going from one place to another ____________________

Using oxygen in the air to gain energy ____________________

Taking in food and water ____________________

Noticing and responding to changes around them ____________________

Making new living things ____________________

Getting rid of materials not needed ____________________

Getting bigger and changing as time passes ____________________

2. Draw lines to match the organs on this list with their position in the body.

heart

brain

large intestine

small intestine

stomach

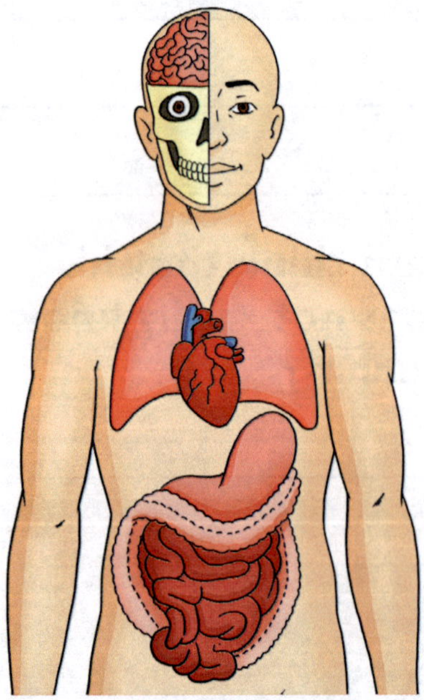

Practising my science language

1. Name each of the organs shown below.
   A list of organ names is provided to help you.

brain kidneys stomach small intestine

large intestine lungs heart

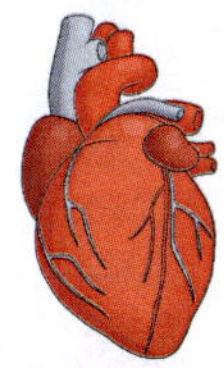

____

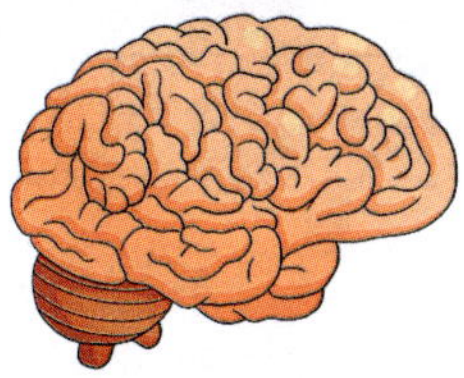

____

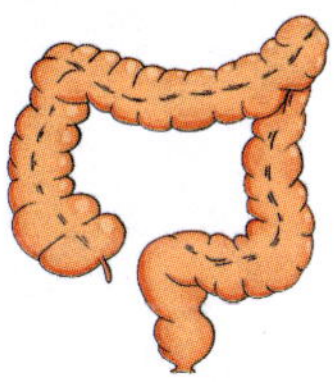

____

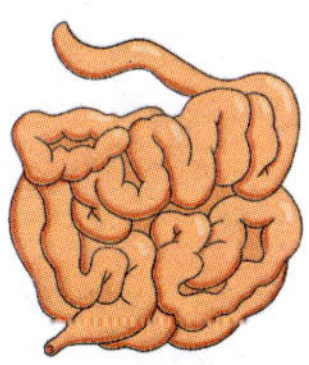

____

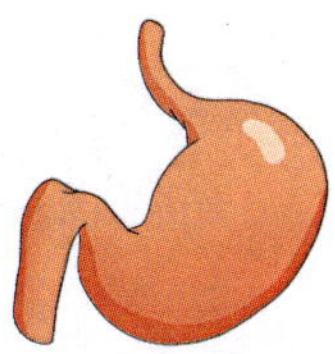

____

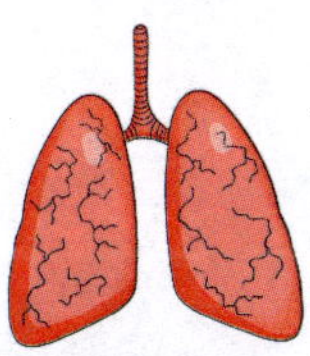

____

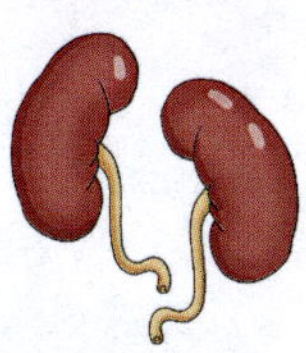

____

Practising my

science language

2. Unscramble the following letters to find the names of the major organs of the human body:

i n r a b ____________________

m a s c o t h ____________________

s l u g n ____________________

e r a t h ____________________

v e l r i ____________________

d i n e s k y ____________________

From school to home

Ask an adult at home to help you ...

1. **Talk to an adult about what you know about the positions of the major organs in your body. Point to where they are inside you. Explain why these major organs are essential in keeping you alive. Practise saying the key words. Use the key words in sentences.**

2. **Now ask someone at home to help you complete the following questions:**

a What did you like about this topic?

____

____

____

b What was hard to understand about this topic?

____

____

____

I understand.

I understand a bit.

I need more time to understand this.

3 **Look at the checklist below. How are you doing now? Circle one face for each statement.**

- I can identify the position of major organs in the body.
- I can explain why the major organs are essential.

4 **Ask an adult at home to read and sign this.**

I have checked learning on this topic.

We have shared some understanding at home.

Signed: ______________________

Date: ______________

Teacher comment: ______________________________

____

Date: ______________

1.2 Body systems and organs

In this second topic in Unit 1 you should be able to describe the functions of the major organs of the body (that is, the stomach, intestines, lungs, kidneys, heart and brain).

You should also be able to name the body system that each major organ belongs to.

Jared and Carissa think they will try to design a robot that uses some of the body systems of a human. Look at their design in the cartoon.

Explain which body systems and organs Jared and Carissa have tried to copy from the human body.

____

____

____

____

Talk with someone at home about the robot. How is it like a human and how is it different from a human?

Check your science!

1. Draw a line to match each of the organs to the job they do in your body.

Organ	Job (function) of organ
stomach	pumps blood around the body, carrying oxygen required for many body processes
kidneys	take in oxygen so it can pass into our blood
liver	allow nutrients and water from food and drink to pass into the blood
heart	breaks down food
brain	filter waste materials from our blood
large and small intestines	has many roles such as helping with digestion and removing harmful chemicals from the blood
lungs	acts as the body's control centre

2. Write the name of the body system that each of the organs belongs to. Choose from the list of body systems below:

nervous   excretory   respiratory   circulatory   digestive

Organ	Body system
heart	______________________
lungs	______________________
kidneys	______________________
stomach, large and small intestines	______________________
brain	______________________

Practising my science language

1. Decide which of the sentences below are true and which are false. Draw a circle around your answer.

   a. Each of your lungs takes in carbon dioxide from the air so it passes into your blood. **True / False**

   b. Your heart pumps blood around the body. The blood carries the oxygen needed all around your body. **True / False**

   c. Your stomach breaks down the food you eat. **True / False**

2. Write the correct versions of any sentences that are false in the space below:

____

____

3. Find the words describing body systems and naming organs in the wordsearch below. Draw a line through each word from the list that you find in the grid.

l	l	e	h	h	d	u	p	t	f	a	e	h	k	s
m	x	n	v	n	g	l	f	u	t	h	o	j	g	n
r	r	i	r	a	r	y	u	x	r	c	z	a	h	v
w	c	a	l	u	n	g	s	w	a	a	c	w	v	n
k	y	r	o	t	e	r	c	x	e	m	m	q	i	e
i	v	b	n	h	j	x	i	a	h	o	d	l	g	r
d	u	y	v	l	h	n	y	x	h	t	d	t	d	v
n	q	e	b	g	n	r	z	l	q	s	s	h	g	o
e	m	z	i	t	d	l	x	p	g	h	r	r	b	u
y	q	u	y	r	o	t	a	l	u	c	r	i	c	s
s	o	n	g	i	e	h	j	d	b	g	f	i	s	m
l	l	u	y	o	y	q	m	l	b	i	z	w	t	y
y	a	r	e	s	p	i	r	a	t	o	r	y	u	r
q	u	o	h	x	e	v	i	t	s	e	g	i	d	d
f	b	o	n	p	a	y	h	y	v	t	q	p	y	u

Hint

The words can go across (forward or backwards), up or down, but not diagonally.

digestive
respiratory
excretory
circulatory
nervous
brain
heart
lungs
kidneys
stomach

From school to home

Ask an adult at home to help you ...

1. **Talk to an adult about what you know about the job that each major organ in your body (the stomach, intestines, lungs, kidneys, heart and brain) does. Explain how these major organs are part of larger organ systems. Use the heart as an example. Practise saying the key words. Use the key words in sentences.**

2. **Now ask someone at home to help you complete the following questions:**

a What did you like about this topic?

____

____

____

b What was hard to understand about this topic?

____

____

____

I understand. I understand a bit. I need more time to understand this.

3 **Look at the checklist below. How are you doing now? Circle one face for each statement.**

- I can describe the functions of the major organs of the body (stomach, intestines, lungs, kidneys, heart and brain).
- I can name the body system each major organ belongs to.

4 **Ask an adult at home to read and sign this.**

I have checked learning on this topic.

We have shared some understanding at home.

Signed: ______________________

Date: ______________

Teacher comment: ______________________________

____

Date: ______________

1.3 When organs go wrong

In this third topic in Unit 1 you should be able to describe why some organs may stop working properly.

You should also be able to describe what, if anything, can be done to treat some problems caused when organs stop working.

Most of Monique's family is fit and healthy. However, sometimes any of them can get ill for a short time.

Which person had the more serious disease – Monique's baby sister or her grandfather?

____

How did Monique's mum make her baby sister feel better?

____

Did Monique's grandfather get better? **Yes** **No**

Who helped him?

____

Check your science!

1. a. Name a disease that can affect your lungs. ______________________

   b. Give two common symptoms of a disease of the lungs.

   ____

   ____

2. Read this information about kidney disease, then answer the questions.

Chronic kidney disease (CKD) is a long-term illness where a person's kidneys do not work properly. Kidney disease is more common in older people. Around one in five men and one in four women aged between 65 and 74 have chronic kidney disease.

The early symptoms of kidney disease may include the following:

In adults:

- passing only small amounts of urine
- fatigue or shortness of breath
- loss of appetite
- very high blood pressure
- very dry, itchy skin.

In children:

- increased fatigue and sleepiness
- decrease in appetite
- poor growth.

With long-term kidney disease, if the kidneys get worse and stop working, there are only two treatment options:

- dialysis, which uses a machine to clean waste products from the blood
- a kidney transplant.

   a. What does CKD stand for? ______________________

   b. If a doctor examined 100 men aged between 65 and 74, how many would you expect to have kidney disease? ______________________

   c. Which symptom of CKD is the same in both children and adults?

   ____

   d. What does dialysis do to the blood of a patient with CKD?

   ____

   e. Besides dialysis, what other treatment can cure CKD?

   ____

Practising my science language

1. a. Fill in the missing letters.

Name a disease that is spread by an insect bite.

m ___ ___ ___ ___ ___ a

b. Name two diseases that are spread by drinking dirty water.

c ___ ___ ___ ___ ___ a and t ___ ___ ___ ___ ___ d

2. Find the words describing some diseases that can affect the human body.

Hint

The words can go across (forward or backwards), up or down, but not diagonally.

measles mumps cancer dementia
polio bronchitis asthma hepatitis
influenza ebola

y	e	f	p	d	e	y	f	d	c	c	g	y	s	o
g	l	i	s	n	d	j	f	n	y	x	a	n	s	m
p	x	l	l	n	o	u	z	x	x	w	p	m	e	o
z	x	y	a	y	h	q	x	q	y	n	f	r	l	e
v	h	a	z	n	e	u	l	f	n	i	p	x	s	n
p	s	g	p	n	w	s	j	l	y	a	u	b	a	p
s	i	t	i	t	a	p	e	h	a	l	o	b	e	y
n	t	u	n	p	w	m	d	l	m	j	d	u	m	i
u	i	t	i	z	i	u	e	o	u	f	b	w	a	t
f	h	f	t	v	f	m	m	t	s	l	l	o	r	w
l	c	v	h	g	e	f	e	l	n	z	d	x	e	d
e	n	m	x	d	k	u	n	i	c	u	t	u	c	k
p	o	l	i	o	a	s	t	h	m	a	p	q	n	u
f	r	r	x	y	p	y	i	a	u	b	j	h	a	x
c	b	r	c	l	m	o	a	l	h	l	p	p	c	p

From school to home

Ask an adult at home to help you ...

1. **Talk to an adult about what you know about how a major organ in your body (for example, the heart) can go wrong and how to treat the diseased organ. Practise saying the key words. Use the key words in sentences.**

2. **Now ask someone at home to help you complete the following questions:**

a What did you like about this topic?

____

____

____

b What was hard to understand about this topic?

____

____

____

I understand. | I understand a bit. | I need more time to understand this.

3 **Look at the checklist below. How are you doing now? Circle one face for each statement.**

- I can describe why some organs may stop working properly.
- I can describe what, if anything, can be done to treat the problems.

4 **Ask an adult at home to read and sign this.**

I have checked learning on this topic.

We have shared some understanding at home.

Signed: ______________________

Date: ______________

Teacher comment: ______________________________

____

Date: ______________

2 Reversible and irreversible changes

2.1 Investigating reversible and irreversible changes

In this first topic in Unit 2 you should be able to distinguish between reversible and irreversible changes, and classify everyday changes as reversible or irreversible.

You should also know about burning as an example of an irreversible change.

Daval is watching his mum boil some eggs in a pan of water for lunch.

This reminds him of his work in school about reversible and irreversible changes.

After eating his lunch, Daval tells his mum about the reversible and irreversible changes happening in the pan when she boiled the eggs.

1. Write down what Daval could say to his mum.

____

____

2. What other ways, besides boiling, can you think of to change eggs by cooking them?

____

____

Discuss your answers with someone who does the cooking at home.

Check your science!

1. Classify the following changes as reversible or irreversible. Circle the correct answer in each example.

a.	Liquid wax flows slowly down the side of a candle and solidifies.	**reversible / irreversible**
b.	Perfume evaporates from an open bottle.	**reversible / irreversible**
c.	A car burns petrol in its engine.	**reversible / irreversible**
d.	A builder mixes cement, sand and small stones with water, pours it into a wooden mould, and leaves it to set hard.	**reversible / irreversible**
e.	Mist forms over a field.	**reversible / irreversible**
f.	An iron nail goes rusty.	**reversible / irreversible**
g.	A baker makes a loaf of bread from a dough mixture in an oven.	**reversible / irreversible**
h.	Ink dries on a piece of paper.	**reversible / irreversible**

2. Explain how heating butter in a pan can cause either a reversible or an irreversible change.

____

____

____

3. Explain why burning a cardboard box is called an irreversible change. Describe any changes you would observe.

____

____

____

Practising my science language

1. Solve the anagram to name the gas needed for materials to burn.

E X N O G Y ______________________

2. Explain the difference between "melting wax" and "burning wax".

Complete the two sentences below:

When wax melts, no new ______________________.

However, when wax burns ______________________.

3. a. Which one of these processes is an irreversible change?

Tick the correct box.

- ☐ melting
- ☐ freezing
- ☐ burning
- ☐ evaporating
- ☐ condensing

b. Fill in the missing letters at the end of this sentence:

All the reversible processes in part a. are changes of s _ _ _ _.

4. Describe what happens in the experiment shown below:

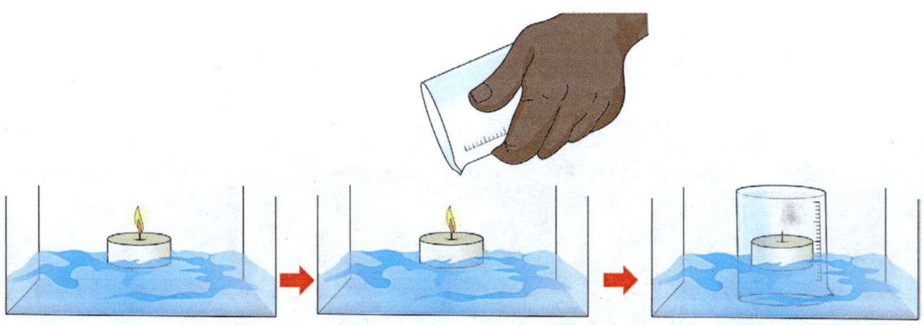

____

____

____

____

From school to home

Ask an adult at home to help you ...

1. **Talk to an adult about what you know about the difference between reversible and irreversible changes. You can use the examples of wood burning and water freezing to explain. Practise saying the key words. Use the key words in sentences.**

2. **Now ask someone at home to help you complete the following questions:**

a What did you like about this topic?

___

___

___

b What was hard to understand about this topic?

___

___

___

I understand. | I understand a bit. | I need more time to understand this.

3 **Look at the checklist below. How are you doing now? Circle one face for each statement.**

- I know how to distinguish between reversible and irreversible changes.
- I can classify everyday changes as reversible or irreversible.
- I know about burning as an example of an irreversible change.

4 **Ask an adult at home to read and sign this.**

I have checked learning on this topic.

We have shared some understanding at home.

Signed: ______________________

Date: ______________

Teacher comment: ______________________________

____

Date: ______________

2.2 Making and separating mixtures

In this second topic in Unit 2 you should be able to observe and record what happens when we mix different solids.

You should also know how to separate mixtures of solids and when to use filtration to separate mixtures.

Andre's little sister is having some fun shaking salt and pepper together on the kitchen table.

Hint

There are paper coffee filters in the kitchen. Salt dissolves in water but pepper does not.

How could Andre get his little sister out of trouble?

Check your science!

1. Zara mixed three different sizes of beads together, labelled as A, B and C in the diagram. She has two sieves (labelled as X and Y) to try to separate the differently sized beads.

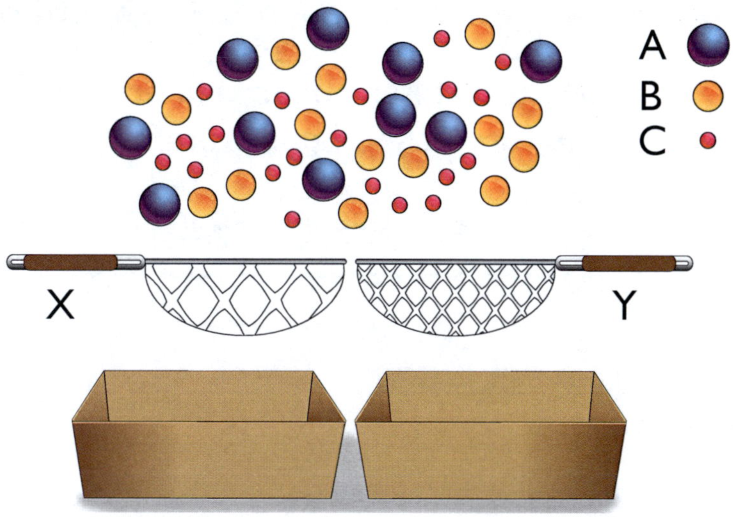

Explain what would be collected in each container beneath sieve X and sieve Y when the mixture of beads was passed through each sieve.

Beneath sieve X:

____

____

Beneath sieve Y:

____

____

2. When you filter a mixture of sugar and sand stirred up in a beaker of water, you use filter paper in a funnel.

Tick the correct box to choose the best explanation of how the filter paper works.

- ☐ The sugar is sticky so it sticks to the filter paper but the sand goes through the paper because it is not sticky.
- ☐ The sugar is made of softer particles than sand so sugar can get through the filter paper, pushed along by the water.
- ☐ The sugar dissolves in water and the tiny dissolved particles of sugar are small enough to fit through the small holes in the filter paper, whereas sand is insoluble and cannot get through the filter paper.

Practising my science language

1. Ling wants to separate a mixture of sand stirred up in water.

   She uses filter paper, a filter funnel, a beaker and a flask to filter the mixture of sand and water.

   a. Draw a labelled diagram of Ling's experiment below:

   b. Explain how the experiment above can separate the sand from the water.

   Fill in the missing words using words from this list:

   water paper sand funnel dissolve holes

   The sand does not ____________________ in the water.

   So the grains of ____________________ are too large to fit through the tiny ____________________ in the filter ____________________.

   The ____________________ passes straight through into the flask below the filter ____________________.

From school to home

Ask an adult at home to help you ...

1. **Talk to an adult about how you can separate solids with differently-sized particles mixed up together. Explain how filtering a mixture can separate a soluble and an insoluble solid. Practise saying the key words. Use the key words in sentences.**

2. **Now ask someone at home to help you complete the following questions:**

a What did you like about this topic?

____

____

____

b What was hard to understand about this topic?

____

____

____

I understand.

I understand a bit.

I need more time to understand this.

3 **Look at the checklist below. How are you doing now? Circle one face for each statement.**

- I can observe and record what happens when we mix solids.
- I know how to separate mixtures of solids.
- I know when to use filtration to separate mixtures.

4 **Ask an adult at home to read and sign this.**

I have checked learning on this topic.

We have shared some understanding at home.

Signed: ______________________

Date: ______________

Teacher comment: ______________________________

____

Date: ______________

2.3 Dissolving

In the units on dissolving you should be able to describe and explain what happens to a solid when it dissolves in a liquid.

You should also be able to explore whether solids are soluble or insoluble, test which is a pure material and which is a mixture, and investigate factors that affect how quickly materials dissolve.

Bastian and Anka have done lots of experiments in school about dissolving materials. But people sometimes have trouble using the word "dissolving"– even Bastian!

1. Why is Bastian puzzled by what his grandmother is telling him?

___

___

2. Why is Anka puzzled by what her grandfather is telling her?

___

___

Check your science!

1. Omar leaves a dish of pure water and a dish of salt solution on a warm windowsill for a week.

   Explain how he could tell which was the dish with the pure water and which was the dish with the salt solution in it.

   ____

   ____

   ____

   ____

2. You are given four powders to see which are soluble in water and which are insoluble.

   You need to make sure you carry out a fair test.

   a. Name two variables you would keep the same when testing each powder.

   ____

   ____

   b. How could you observe which powders were soluble and which were insoluble in water?

   ____

   ____

   ____

   ____

   c. How would you present your results?

   Tick the correct box.

   ☐ a table

   ☐ a table and a bar chart

   ☐ a table and a line graph

Check your science!

3. Ravit and Layla are investigating sugar dissolving. They want to find out how the temperature of the water affects the time it takes the sugar to dissolve.

a. Name four measuring instruments they could use when carrying out their tests. Write down what each instrument measures.

Measuring instrument	What does it measure?

b. Write down a prediction for their investigation.

Practising my science language

1. A group investigated how the temperature of water affected the time it took sugar to dissolve.

   Look at this line graph of their results:

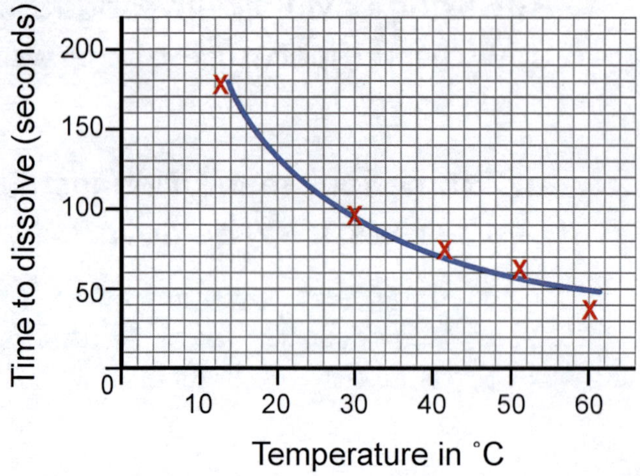

   a. Use the graph to answer this question. How long did the sugar take to dissolve at 30 °C? ______ seconds

   b. If the temperature is low, what happens to the time it takes the sugar to dissolve? Finish the sentence.

   When the temperature is low, ______________________________

   ______________________________.

   c. If the temperature is high, what happens to the time it takes the sugar to dissolve? Finish the sentence.

   When the temperature is high, ______________________________

   ______________________________.

   d. How does the time it takes sugar to dissolve depend on the temperature? Complete the pattern.

   The higher the temperature, ______________________________

   ______________________________.

   e. The whole class were doing the same investigation.
   The teacher noticed that another group tested sugar grains at three different temperatures and a sugar cube at another two different temperatures.
   What did this group do wrong? Complete the sentence.

   The group should have ______________________________

   ______________________________.

From school to home

Ask an adult at home to help you ...

1. **Talk to an adult about what you know about what might happen when solids are added to water. Discuss the factors that affect how quickly sugar dissolves in water. Practise saying the key words. Use the key words in sentences.**

2. **Now ask someone at home to help you complete the following questions:**

a What did you like about this topic?

____

____

____

b What was hard to understand about this topic?

____

____

____

I understand. I understand a bit. I need more time to understand this.

3 **Look at the checklist below. How are you doing now? Circle one face for each statement.**

- I can observe, record and begin to explain the changes that take place when some solids are added to water.
- I know that some solids dissolve in water to form solutions and others are insoluble.
- I can test which is a pure material and which is a mixture.
- I can investigate factors that affect how quickly materials dissolve.

4 **Ask an adult at home to read and sign this.**

I have checked learning on this topic.

We have shared some understanding at home.

Signed: ______________________

Date: ______________

Teacher comment: ______________________________

____

Date: ______________

3 Food chains

3.1 Living things in their habitat

In this first topic in Unit 3 you should know how to identify living things in a habitat using a key.

You should also know how plants and animals depend on each other in their habitat.

Haru is watching TV with his dad when a programme about habitats comes on.

Haru has just been studying different habitats in science lessons.

1. Haru has to explain what "habitat" means to his dad. What will he say?

____

____

2. The programme on "Habitats around the World" looks at a tropical rainforest first. Describe the main plant life you would expect to find in a tropical rainforest.

____

____

____

Discuss your answers and some other habitats with an adult.

Check your science!

Deena did a survey of the animals in her garden habitat.

Here are the creatures she found there:

Deena used the key below to identify each creature.

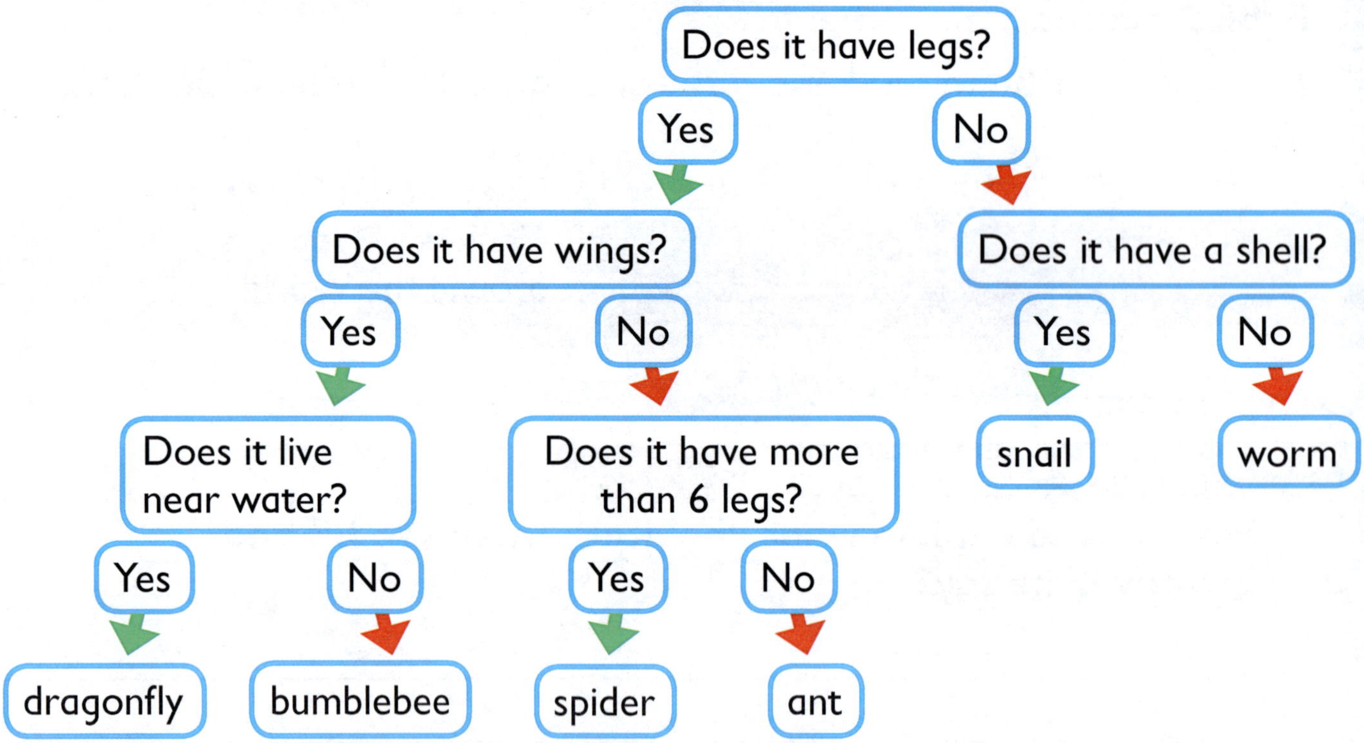

Identify the creatures **A** to **F**.

A is ______________________.

B is ______________________.

C is ______________________.

D is ______________________.

E is ______________________.

F is ______________________.

Practising my science language

1. What do we call the environment in which certain plants and animals live? Solve the anagram to find the answer.

   t h i b a t a = ___ ___ ___ ___ ___ ___ ___

2. A class collects a variety of leaves from different types of trees. What can they use to identify the trees that the leaves came from?

   ____

3. Read this information, then answer the questions about it.

> Animals and plants living in the same habitat depend on each other to survive. For example, animals can help to spread (disperse) seeds. This makes sure that seeds can start growing some distance from their parent plant. Some seeds are spiky and stick to the fur of passing animals. Other seeds are eaten by animals and are then passed out in the animals' faeces (poo).
>
> It is important for the young plants to grow some distance away from their parent plant. This reduces competition for light, water and nutrients. It is good for both the new plant and the parent plant.

   a. What does the word "disperse" mean?

   ____

   b. What three things do plants compete for in order to survive?

   ____

   c. The third sentence in the information starts "This makes sure that seeds can start growing ...".
   What do we call this process when seeds start to grow?
   The first letter is given.

   G______________________________

   d. Underline two sentences in the information that describe how animals can help spread the seeds of some plants.

Practising my science language

4. Draw a key that can be used to identify a worm, a mouse and an eagle in the space below:

From school to home

Ask an adult at home to help you ...

1. Talk to an adult about what you know about using a key to identify things and explain to them how the living things in a habitat depend on each other to survive. Practise saying the key words. Use the key words in sentences.

2. Now ask someone at home to help you complete the following questions:

a What did you like about this topic?

____

____

____

b What was hard to understand about this topic?

____

____

____

I understand. I understand a bit. I need more time to understand this.

3 **Look at the checklist below. How are you doing now? Circle one face for each statement.**

- I can use a key to identify living things in a habitat.
- I know how plants and animals depend on each other in their habitats.

4 **Ask an adult at home to read and sign this.**

I have checked learning on this topic.

We have shared some understanding at home.

Signed: ______________________

Date: ______________

Teacher comment: ______________________________

____

Date: ______________

3.2 Food chains

In this second topic in Unit 3 you should know what food chains represent and how to show food chains in writing and in diagrams.

You should also know that food chains always start with a plant.

1. Describe what is happening in these three pictures.

____

____

____

2. What gets passed along the food chain going from left to right?

____

____

____

3. If you draw your own cartoon to show a food chain, what should always be in your first picture?

____

____

____

Check your science!

1. Sort the following lists of living things into their food chains.

   a. wheat eagle rat

   Food chain:

   ____

   b. blackbird leafy bush hawk caterpillar

   Food chain:

   ____

   c. toad snake grass grasshopper

   Food chain:

   ____

   d. squid penguin seal seaweed crab whale

   Food chain:

   ____

2. **a.** Which one of the food chains in Question 1 takes place in the sea?

   Tick the correct box.

   - [ ] part a
   - [ ] part b
   - [ ] part c
   - [ ] part d

   b. List the four living things that start each of the food chains in parts **a** to **d** in Question 1.

   ______________ ______________

   ______________ ______________

   c. What do all these living things listed in part **b** have in common?

   ____

   ____

Practising my science language

1. Errol's computer has a fault and has mixed up the letters of each living thing in the following food chains.

   Can you help him to correct the food chains?

   a. mzaie ⇨ oumse ⇨ low

   ______ ⇨ ______ ⇨ ______

   b. elaga ⇨ ringher ⇨ doc ⇨ elas

   ______ ⇨ ______ ⇨ ______ ⇨ ______

   c. Find all the living things from the food chains in parts (a) and (b) above in this wordsearch:

p	t	z	j	a	b	e	z	i	a	m	c
b	h	u	g	w	r	g	a	q	h	h	k
p	e	g	e	y	o	i	e	c	j	l	o
e	r	d	s	m	r	m	g	j	c	k	z
a	r	o	k	t	l	y	i	z	m	b	j
g	i	c	q	a	n	r	l	o	w	l	s
l	n	k	t	z	z	e	s	u	o	m	e
a	g	g	a	b	p	q	k	o	m	l	a
f	p	a	p	z	r	q	f	k	z	k	l
k	y	c	e	s	u	s	f	f	d	s	f
i	g	h	m	u	c	k	j	g	s	h	i
w	l	q	v	l	h	m	o	r	v	x	y

2. Choose words from the list below to complete the information about how plants get their energy at the start of a food chain.

   photosynthesis water Sun leaves sugar

   Plants can make their own food. They can take in energy from the ______ in a process called ______. This takes place mainly in a plant's ______.

   A series of chemical reactions take place which can be shown as:

   sunlight

   carbon dioxide + ______ ⇨ ______ + oxygen

   (an energy store)

From school to home

Ask an adult at home to help you ...

1. **Talk to an adult about what " food chains" are and how you can show these in words and diagrams. Practise saying the key words. Use the key words in sentences.**

2. **Now ask someone at home to help you complete the following questions:**

a What did you like about this topic?

____

____

____

b What was hard to understand about this topic?

____

____

____

I understand. I understand a bit. I need more time to understand this.

3 **Look at the checklist below. How are you doing now? Circle one face for each statement.**

- I know what food chains represent.
- I can show food chains in writing and diagrams.
- I know that food chains always begin with a plant.

4 **Ask an adult at home to read and sign this.**

I have checked learning on this topic.

We have shared some understanding at home.

Signed: ______________________

Date: ______________

Teacher comment: ______________________________

____

Date: ______________

3.3 Explaining food chains

In the third topic in Unit 3 you should be able to explain why food chains always begin with a plant and what the words producer, consumer, predator and prey mean. You should also be able to find the food chains in food webs.

The rabbits in a habitat have picked up a nasty disease. Look at the animal hospital below then answer the questions:

1. Why are the foxes worried that the rabbits will die out?

____

____

2. The rabbits feed on grass in this food chain. List the living things in a food chain in the rabbit's habitat.

____

____

Discuss the cartoon with an adult.

Check your science!

1. Look at the tiger in this picture:

a. Describe the features that make a tiger an effective predator.

____

____

____

b. What is the name given to animals that predators hunt and eat?

____

c. List some useful features that could help an animal survive when it is hunted by a predator.

____

____

____

2. Here is a simple food web:

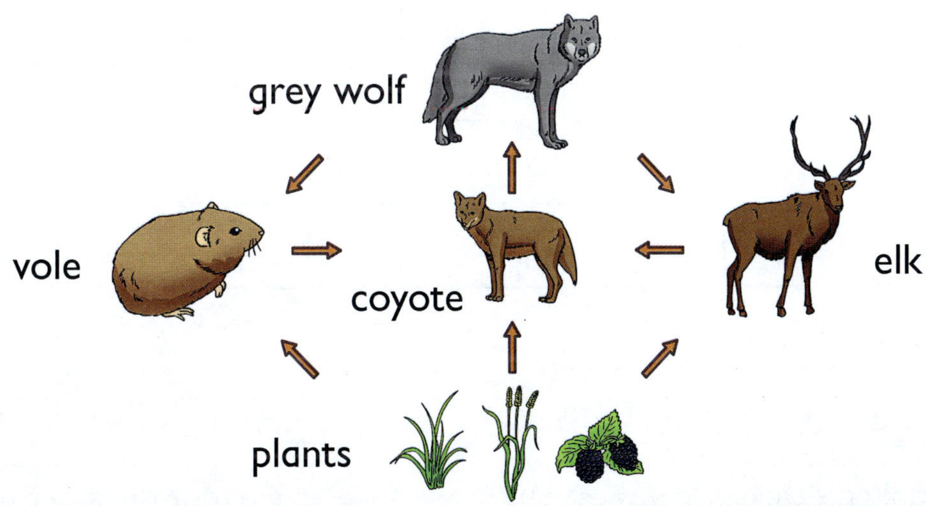

a. Draw a food chain with three living things from this food web.

____

b. Draw a food chain with four living things from this food web.

____

Practising my science language

1. Fill in the missing letters.

a. What do we call all the food chains in a habitat, combined in one diagram?

A f_ _ _ w_ _

b. What flows through a food chain in the direction of the arrows?

E_ _ _ _ _

c. What do we find at the start of all food chains?

A p_ _ _ _

2. Complete the crossword using key words from this unit.

Across

3. The animals that follow the plant in a food chain

5. An animal that hunts and eats another animal

Down

1. The plant at the start of a food chain

2. Animal that is eaten by a predator

4. The source of all the energy in a food chain

From school to home

Ask an adult at home to help you ...

1. **Talk to an adult about what you know about producers, consumers, predators and prey in food chains. Explain what a food web is. Practise saying the key words. Use the key words in sentences.**

2. **Now ask someone at home to help you complete the following questions:**

a What did you like about this topic?

____

____

____

b What was hard to understand about this topic?

____

____

____

I understand. I understand a bit. I need more time to understand this.

3 **Look at the checklist below. How are you doing now? Circle one face for each statement.**

- I can explain why food chains always begin with a plant.
- I can identify and explain in food chains the terms:
  - producer
  - consumer
  - predator
  - prey.
- I can identify the food chains in food webs.

4 **Ask an adult at home to read and sign this.**

I have checked learning on this topic.

We have shared some understanding at home.

Signed: ______________________

Date: ______________

Teacher comment: ______________________________

____

Date: ______________

4 Electrical conductors and insulators

4.1 Circuit diagrams

In this first topic in Unit 4 you should know the symbols of common electrical components.

You should also be able to represent a circuit using circuit diagrams.

It is past Akmal's bedtime but he is reading an exciting story with the help of his torch.

This diagram shows what is inside Akmal's torch.

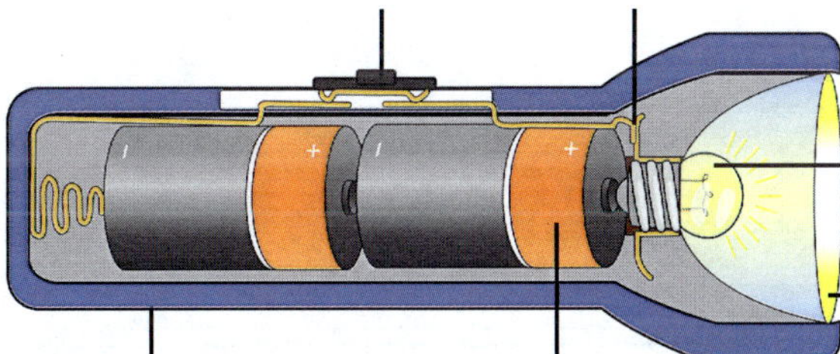

Akmal's torch has two cells (batteries), a switch, a bulb and connectors.

In the space alongside draw a circuit diagram for the torch.

Explain your circuit diagram to an adult at home.

Check your science!

1. Draw the symbols for the parts of a circuit to complete the table below:

Part of circuit	Standard symbol
One cell	
Two cells or a battery (some people call a single cell a "battery" too)	
Wire	
Bulb (also called lamp)	
Switch	

2. In the space below, draw a circuit diagram showing a circuit made up of:

- three cells
- one switch
- four bulbs.

Practising my science language

1. Complete the following crossword about electrical circuits.

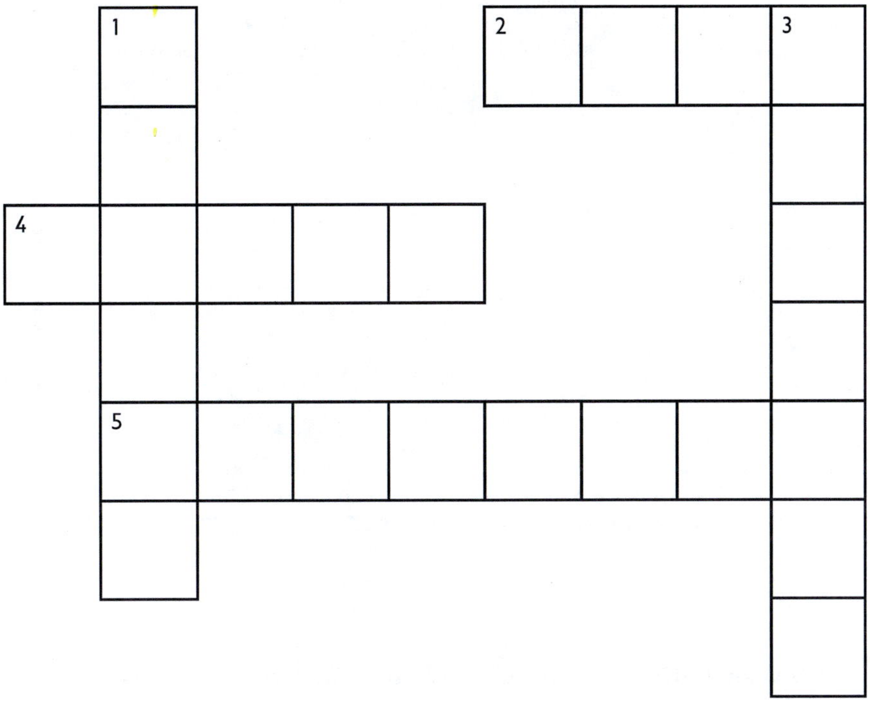

Across

2. This part of a circuit gives off light when electricity passes through it.

4. These connect different parts of an electrical circuit.

5. For an electric current to flow around a circuit, the circuit must be _ _ _ _ _ _ _ _ _.

Down

1. This part of a circuit completes or breaks the circuit.

3. This is a series of cells joined together in a circuit to produce a higher voltage.

Practising my science language

2. Look at this diagram of a simple circuit:

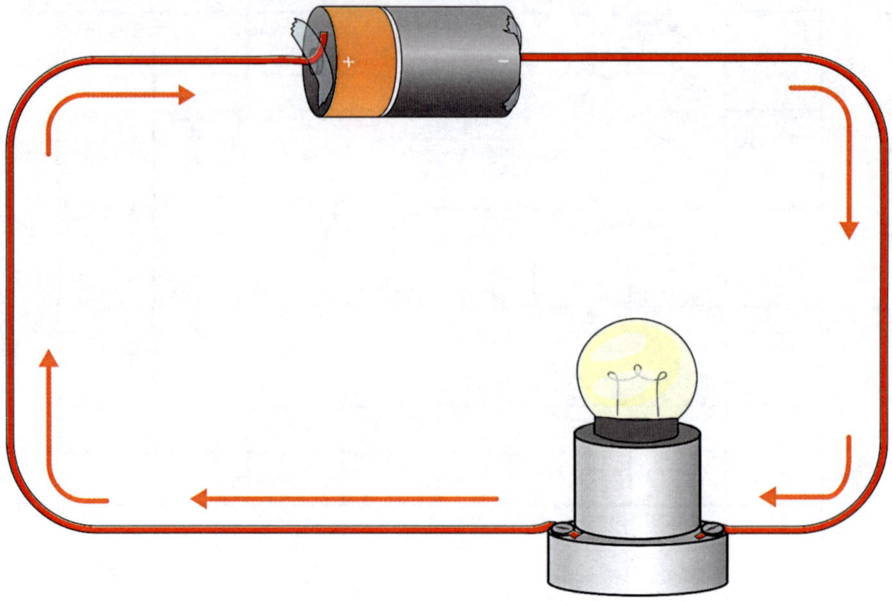

a. Draw the circuit diagram in the space below.

b. Explain what is happening in the circuit.

____

____

____

Hint

Use the clues in the crossword on page 51 to help you explain.

From school to home

Ask an adult at home to help you ...

1. **Talk to an adult about what you know about the symbols of common electrical components and how to represent circuits using circuit diagrams. Practise saying the key words. Use the key words in sentences.**

2. **Now ask someone at home to help you complete the following questions:**

a What did you like about this topic?

____

____

____

b What was hard to understand about this topic?

____

____

____

I understand. | I understand a bit. | I need more time to understand this.

3 **Look at the checklist below. How are you doing now? Circle one face for each statement.**

- I know the symbols of common electrical components.
- I can represent a circuit using a circuit diagram.

4 **Ask an adult at home to read and sign this.**

I have checked learning on this topic.

We have shared some understanding at home.

Signed: ______________________

Date: ______________

Teacher comment: ______________________________

____

Date: ______________

4.2 Conductors and insulators

In this topic you should be able to investigate how some materials are better conductors of electricity than others and to classify materials as good electrical conductors or insulators.

You should also know how insulators are used in everyday items to keep us safe from electricity and why metals and plastics are used to make plugs and switches.

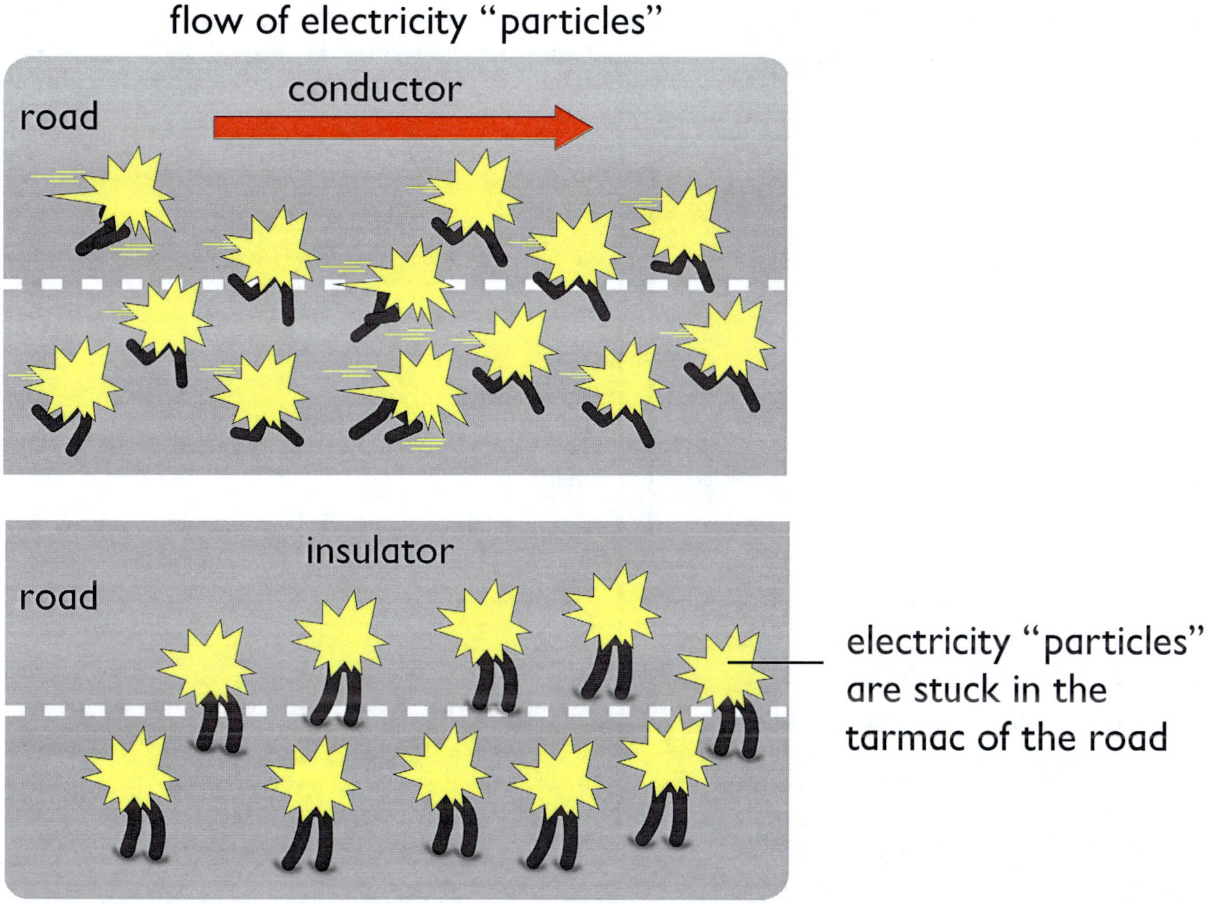

How do the cartoons above show the difference between electrical conductors and insulators?

____

____

____

Discuss which materials are electrical conductors and which are electrical insulators with an adult at home.

Check your science!

1. Brianna is trying to find out which materials let electricity pass through them and which do not. She has the equipment shown here to test different materials:

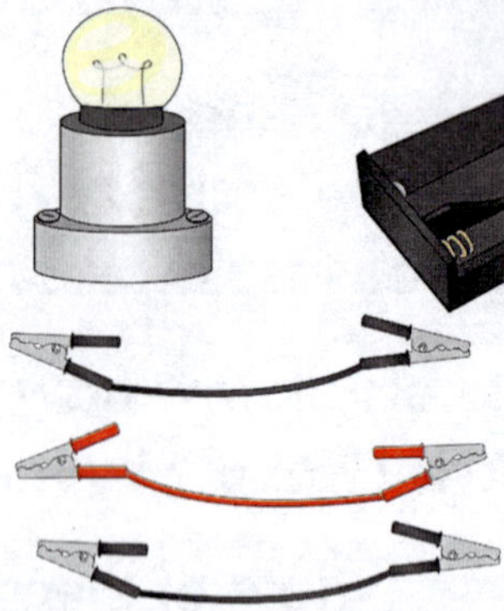

   a. Finish off the drawing of an electrical circuit Brianna could use to test the materials:

   b. Now draw a circuit diagram of the circuit in part **a**:

2. a. Which three of the following materials are electrical insulators?

   Tick the correct boxes.

☐	gold	☐	iron
☐	rubber	☐	nylon
☐	paper	☐	brass

   b. Which material in the list above is the electrical conductor often used to make the pins in a plug that slot into a socket?

   ____

Practising my science language

1. a. Riya is thinking about a list of electrical conductors.

Unscramble the letters to name the electrical conductors.

1. ______________________
2. ______________________
3. ______________________
4. ______________________
5. ______________________

b. Gavin is thinking about a list of electrical insulators.

Unscramble the letters to name the electrical insulators.

1. ______________________
2. ______________________
3. ______________________

2. Explain why copper is used inside an electric cable but plastic is used around the outside by finishing these two sentences:

Copper is used inside a wire because ______________________

____.

Wires have a plastic coating because they are ______________________ so people handling the wire when it is in a circuit do not

____.

From school to home

Ask an adult at home to help you ...

1. **Talk to an adult about electrical conductors and insulators, then explain how they are used in plugs and switches. Practise saying the key words. Use the key words in sentences.**

2. **Now ask someone at home to help you complete the following questions:**

a What did you like about this topic?

____

____

____

b What was hard to understand about this topic?

____

____

____

I understand. I understand a bit. I need more time to understand this.

3 **Look at the checklist below. How are you doing now? Circle one face for each statement.**

- I can investigate how some materials are better conductors of electricity than others.
- I can classify materials as good conductors of electricity or as electrical insulators.
- I can explain why metals and plastics are used to make plugs and switches.

4 **Ask an adult at home to read and sign this.**

I have checked learning on this topic.

We have shared some understanding at home.

Signed: ______________________

Date: ______________

Teacher comment: ____________________________

____

Date: ______________

4.3 Investigating circuits

In this last topic in the unit you should be able to predict and test the effects of making changes to circuits.

You should also be able to investigate how the length (or thickness) of a wire affects the flow of electricity around a circuit.

What should Nissa say to her brother to explain what is happening inside the cable?

Hint

Is there really just one wire going into the plug and the TV?

____

____

____

____

Discuss the cartoon with an adult.

Check your science!

1. Faris and Tori were investigating what affects how brightly a bulb shines.

   They set up these circuits and then judged the brightness of the bulb in each test.

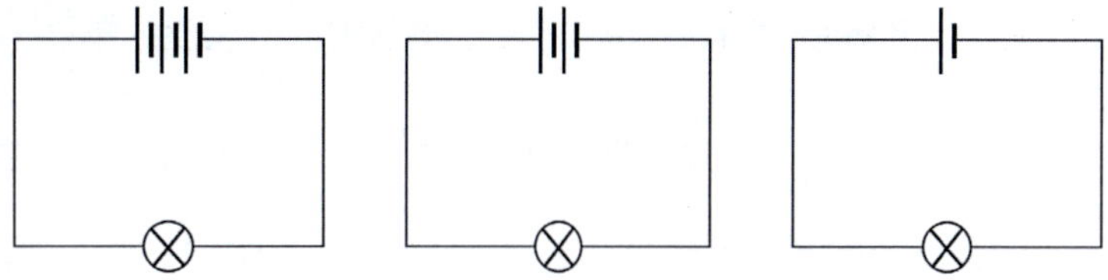

bright normal dim

   a. What variable did Faris and Tori change between each test?

   ___

   b. What can Faris and Tori conclude from these three tests? What is the pattern?

   ___

   ___

2. Faris and Tori then tested another three circuits:

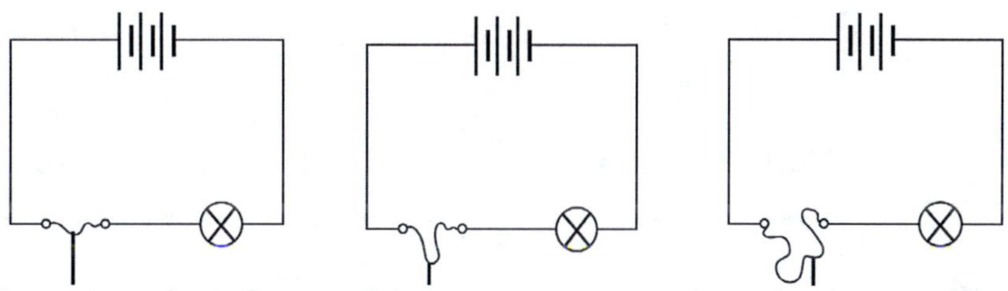

thin wire bright thin wire normal thin wire dim

   a. What variable did Faris and Tori change between each test with the wire?

   ___

   b. What can Faris and Tori conclude from these three tests with the thin wire? What is the pattern?

   ___

   ___

   c. Which two variables need to be the same when testing the wire?

   ___ and ___

   d. Why do these variables need to be kept the same?

   ___

   e. What would Faris and Tori have to measure so that their results could be shown on a line graph?

   ___

Practising my science language

You want to find out which factors affect the brightness of a bulb.

1. Write down a list of variables (factors) that might affect how brightly a bulb shines.

____

____

2. Now choose one factor from your list to test. ________________

   Predict what will happen. Finish this sentence.

   I think that ____

   ____.

3. Plan a fair test that you could carry out in class to see if your prediction is correct.
   Include a circuit diagram in your answer.

4. Make a list of the equipment you would need to do your test.

____

____

From school to home

Ask an adult at home to help you ...

1. **Talk to an adult about what you know about investigating what affects the brightness of a bulb in an electrical circuit. Practise saying the key words. Use the key words in sentences.**

2. **Now ask someone at home to help you complete the following questions:**

a What did you like about this topic?

____

____

____

b What was hard to understand about this topic?

____

____

____

I understand. I understand a bit. I need more time to understand this.

3 **Look at the checklist below. How are you doing now? Circle one face for each statement.**

- I can predict and test the effects of making changes to circuits.
- I can investigate how the length (or thickness) of a wire affects how well it conducts electricity.

4 **Ask an adult at home to read and sign this.**

I have checked learning on this topic.

We have shared some understanding at home.

Signed: ______________________

Date: _____________

Teacher comment: ____________________________

____

Date: _____________

5 Caring for the environment

5.1 Spaceship Earth – the atmosphere

This topic looks at some of the challenges facing the Earth's atmosphere. By the end of this first topic in Unit 5 you should be able to describe how humans are polluting the air and how pollution from burning fuels causes acid rain.

You should also be able to explain that carbon dioxide is increasing the greenhouse effect.

Tomi and Jessica are talking about the Earth.

1. What does Tomi mean when he says "The whole Earth is our habitat"?

____

____

2. What do you do to look after your home? How do you help?

____

____

Check your science!

1. Mrs Ling was talking to Miss Jean-Baptiste. People often get confused by science.

a. What would you say to Mrs Ling to help her understand about acid rain?

____

____

b. Miss Jean-Baptiste thinks that there is gas in her greenhouse. What would you say to her?

____

____

2. If you were in charge of a country, what laws would you make to help to improve the environment?

____

____

____

Practising my
science language

1. How confident are you that you could explain the meaning of these words? Try to explain them to someone at home and then tick the boxes to show how confident you are.

	Very confident	Probably okay	Not very sure
Your environment			
A habitat			
Carbon dioxide			
Acid rain			
Greenhouse effect			

If you have ticked "Not very sure", ask an adult at home to explain them to you.

2. Have you done anything to help save Planet Earth?
Tick below if you have:

- ☐ picked up litter
- ☐ turned off unwanted lights
- ☐ walked instead of being driven
- ☐ recycled some materials
- ☐ helped an animal
- ☐ planted something
- ☐ tidied your room

3. Circle the words you would use to describe the environment you live in.

tidy clean safe warm cold friendly country city town

village polluted quiet noisy busy smelly dirty

4. What two things would you like to see happen to improve your environment?

____

____

From school to home

Ask an adult at home to help you ...

1. **Talk to an adult about what you know about how humans are polluting the air and how pollution from burning fuels causes acid rain. You should also be able to explain the greenhouse effect and how carbon dioxide from human activities affects it. Practise saying the key words. Use the key words in sentences.**

2. **Now ask someone at home to help you complete the following questions:**

a What did you like about this topic?

____

____

____

b What was hard to understand about this topic?

____

____

____

I understand. I understand a bit. I need more time to understand this.

3 **Look at the checklist below. How are you doing now? Circle one face for each statement.**

- I can describe ways in which pollution is harming the atmosphere.
- I can explain what is meant by acid rain.
- I can explain how the greenhouse effect works.

4 **Ask an adult at home to read and sign this.**

I have checked learning on this topic.

We have shared some understanding at home.

Signed: ______________________

Date: ______________

Teacher comment: ______________________________

____

Date: ______________

5.2 Spaceship Earth – habitats and buildings

This topic considers the importance of habitats to wildlife. It looks at the challenge of building new homes for people while also respecting habitats for wildlife.

By the end of this second topic in Unit 5 you should know how important green spaces are for healthy living and about ways to ensure that enough habitats remain for living things.

You should also know about deforestation and how it is harming habitats.

Everybody should have a place to live but a new building can mean losing a habitat.

1. **Think of a natural habitat near your home. What animals live there?**

____

____

2. **Towns and buildings are planned by architects. What would you say to them to make sure that wildlife habitats are cared for?**

I would tell them ____

____

____

Check your science!

1. Here are three families. They each need a home. How can a new town provide them all with a good home? You can draw or write your answer in the space below.

2. Arvi's uncle owns a large forest in Brazil. The forest covers 1000 square kilometres.

   a. Write down the types of wildlife which you think might be living in the forest. Can you think of ten different species?

   ____

   ____

   b. Arvi's uncle wants to destroy the forest so that he can grow soya as animal food for cattle. This is worrying Arvi. Write a short email to Arvi's uncle to help him understand how important forests are.

   Dear Arvi's uncle,

   ____

   ____

   ____

   ____

   ____

Practising my science language

1. Why is it important to have green spaces as well as homes and shops? Do you agree or disagree with these reasons? Tick your answers.

	Agree	Disagree
Green spaces are full of flowers. They look nice.		
Plants give off oxygen.		
Without habitats, animals might die.		
People need to walk, cycle and enjoy fresh air.		
Children can learn about wildlife.		

2. Good town planners will allow for some "green space" in their plans. Draw what a green space might look like. Explain your drawing.

3. The world's tiger population is slowly decreasing. Their habitats are being destroyed and illegal hunting is killing them. One day there may be no tigers left in the wild.

   How can we help to save the world's tigers? Think of three ideas and write them below.

1. ______________________________

2. ______________________________

3. ______________________________

From school to home

Ask an adult at home to help you ...

1. **Talk to an adult about what you know about how to make sure that enough habitats remain for living things. Tell them about deforestation and how it is harming important habitats. Practise saying the key words. Use the key words in sentences.**

2. **Now ask someone at home to help you complete the following questions:**

a What did you like about this topic?

____

____

____

b What was hard to understand about this topic?

____

____

____

I understand. I understand a bit. I need more time to understand this.

3 **Look at the checklist below. How are you doing now? Circle one face for each statement.**

- I know how natural habitats can become threatened by town and city developing.
- I know how important forests are for wildlife.
- I have researched how forests and wildlife can be protected.

4 **Ask an adult at home to read and sign this.**

I have checked learning on this topic.

We have shared some understanding at home.

Signed: ______________________

Date: ______________

Teacher comment: ______________________________

____

Date: ______________

5.3 Spaceship Earth – save energy and recycle

This topic looks at how energy is provided and how energy supply can affect the environment. It considers the concept of "green energy" and also how to save energy.

By the end of this third topic in Unit 5 you will know about the importance of saving fossil fuels for the future.

You will also know that recycling waste can save energy and how waste can be recycled.

We can use many old materials again. Have you seen collection bins for recycled materials?

1. What new things can be made from:

a. old metal objects?

____

b. old plastic bags?

____

2. Old glass can be melted to make glass for new bottles. What happens to old paper? How is old paper made into something useful?

____

____

____

Check your science!

1. Which of the following are fossil fuels? Circle your answers.

wind coal sunshine gas uranium

paper oil water leaves

2. Name two things that can be made from:

   a. recycled paper and card

   ____

   ____

   b. recycled glass.

   ____

   ____

3. Oil can provide energy in a power station. Name three other uses for oil.

   1. ______________________________
   2. ______________________________
   3. ______________________________

4. Errol did a waste project at his school. His class collected waste for four weeks and then measured what they had collected. Here are the results.

glass 4.5 kg	plastic 2.0 kg	cardboard 5.5 kg
metal 3.0 kg	paper 8.5 kg	other 3 kg

   a. Create a bar chart or pictogram to show these amounts of waste.

   b. What was the total mass of the waste collected over four weeks? ________

Practising my science language

1. Why are we encouraged to sort our waste?

   Decide if you agree or disagree with these statements about sorting waste. Tick your answer.

	Agree	Disagree
We sort waste so it can be buried in separate places.		
We sort waste so that it is lighter to lift when taken away.		
Some materials can be recycled.		
Recycling is easier if materials are not mixed.		
Recycling waste saves energy.		

2. Select words from the list to complete the following passage.

   atmosphere recycling carbon dioxide oil
   energy fossil fuels Plastics Earth

   Using a material for a second time is called ________________. This process saves ________________. Many power stations produce energy by burning ________________. These power stations release ________________ into the ________________. Cars and planes use fuel which comes from ________________. ________________ also come from oil. The oil below the surface of the ________________ will run out one day.

3. Mr Johnson lives near Anissa. Mr Johnson does not sort his waste and he refuses to recycle any waste. This worries Anissa. Help Anissa to write a letter to Mr Johnson on a separate page to explain why he should recycle his waste.

From school to home

Ask an adult at home to help you ...

1. **Talk to an adult about what you know about saving fossil fuels for the future and about recycling. Practise saying the key words. Use the key words in sentences.**

2. **Now ask someone at home to help you complete the following questions:**

a What did you like about this topic?

____

____

____

b What was hard to understand about this topic?

____

____

____

I understand.

I understand a bit.

I need more time to understand this.

3 **Look at the checklist below. How are you doing now? Circle one face for each statement.**

- I know what fossil fuels are.
- I know that the Earth's fossil fuels are running out.
- I can describe the types of waste that we produce from our homes.
- I can explain what is meant by recycling.

4 **Ask an adult at home to read and sign this.**

I have checked learning on this topic.

We have shared some understanding at home.

Signed: ______________________

Date: _____________

Teacher comment: ____________________________

____

Date: _____________

5.4 Spaceship Earth – taking care of my local environment

Developing a sense of responsibility for the planet begins at home and in school. These are your local environments. This section considers how we can act in our local environment to help the Earth.

By the end of this fourth topic in Unit 5 you should know how to reduce litter and waste in and around the school and about how your school can use less energy.

You should also know about how habitats near your school can be protected.

Kassim and Vinesh are worried about the Earth. They want to help. But how can just two people make a difference?

1. What things are you responsible for in your life? Tick your answers.

Getting to school on time	☐	**Doing shopping**	☐
Washing yourself	☐	**Caring for another person**	☐
Cleaning dishes	☐	**Looking after an animal**	☐

2. Think about the future. How can the world be a better place for everyone?

____

____

____

3. When you are older, what do you hope to do to help the Earth?

____

____

____

Check your science!

1. Kiri and Alisha completed a litter survey. Here are some of their results written as a list:

   plastic: 2.5 kg; paper: 4 kg; card: 1 kg; glass: 0.5 kg; metal: 0 kg.

   Make a chart or graph on a piece of paper to show these results.

2. Alec and Janya did a lights survey in school one summer day. They counted the number of lights that were switched on each hour. Their results are on this bar chart.

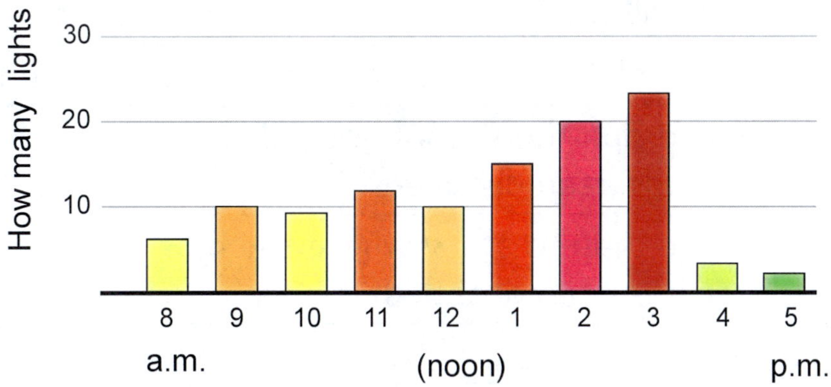

   a. How many lights were being used at noon? ______________________

   b. When were most lights used? ______________________

   c. Why were so few lights used after 4 p.m.? ______________________

   d. How would this chart look different if they did their survey in the winter?

   ____

3. Describe one habitat that you have studied. Include information about:
   - where the habitat is
   - which animals or plants live there
   - why the habitat is suitable for these animals/plants.

____

____

____

____

Practising my science language

1. Tick the actions below that will save energy for your school.

Opening all the windows	
Switching off unwanted lights	
Recycling waste paper	

Using LED light bulbs	
Stopping draughts	
Turning off hot water taps	

2. Rafi and Amira were planning to do a litter survey. Here is their plan.

Step 1	Count all the litter bins inside the school.
Step 2	Count all the litter bins outside the school.
Step 3	Collect all the litter on the ground and put it into the bins.
Step 4	Photograph the school grounds to show where the stray litter has been dropped.
Step 5	Make a map to show where the bins are and where the litter has been dropped.
Step 6	

a. Which step is in the wrong order? Explain why.

____

____

b. What should they do in Step 6?

____

____

3. Leena's school held an environment afternoon. Local people were invited and 120 people attended. A collection raised some money to improve the school environment. Your teacher has asked you to write a letter to say thank you to Mrs Anand, the local shopkeeper who helped with cakes during the event. Complete a short thank-you letter to Mrs Anand on a separate page explaining why her help is important to the school environment.

From school to home

Ask an adult at home to help you ...

1. **Talk to an adult about what you know about ways to reduce litter and waste in and around the school and ways that your school can use less energy. Discuss the ways habitats around your school can be protected. Practise saying the key words. Use the key words in sentences.**

2. **Now ask someone at home to help you complete the following questions:**

a What did you like about this topic?

____

____

____

b What was hard to understand about this topic?

____

____

____

I understand. I understand a bit. I need more time to understand this.

3 **Look at the checklist below. How are you doing now? Circle one face for each statement.**

- I know about ways my school and home can save energy.
- I have investigated ideas for recycling in my school.
- I have made observations, measurements and completed surveys.
- I can describe the location and nature of habitats in and around my school.
- I can list some of the animals that use these local habitats.
- I can describe how a habitat can be improved.

4 **Ask an adult at home to read and sign this.**

I have checked learning on this topic.

We have shared some understanding at home.

Signed: ______________________

Date: ______________

Teacher comment: ______________________________

____

Date: ______________

6 Mass and weight

6.1 Investigating mass and weight

By the end of this first topic in Unit 6 you should be able to explain the difference between the mass and the weight of an object, and to use a forcemeter to measure weight.

You should also be able to use the units of force (including weight) and mass, as well as calculate the weight of an object when you know its mass.

Jayesh's father has been on a diet. His doctor told him he had to lose some weight because it was putting his heart under strain. Jayesh's father ate less and exercised more for two months, then went back to see his doctor.

Jayesh's father tells him about his second visit to the doctor when he gets home. He says that the doctor told him, "Good, your weight has gone down to 95 kilograms."

Jayesh says that he has just learnt about the difference between mass and weight in school.

Suggest two ways that Jayesh could correct what the doctor said to make it more scientifically accurate.

Hint

Use a different unit of measurement.

1. **By changing the word "weight" in what the doctor said to:**

____

2. **By changing the "95 kilograms" in what the doctor said to:**

____

Check your science!

1. Which one of the following correctly describes what gravity is?

   Tick the correct box below:

   ☐ An arrow that points towards the centre of the Earth

   ☐ A mass that acts towards the centre of the Earth

   ☐ A force that acts towards the centre of the Earth

   ☐ A force that acts upwards from the centre of the Earth

2. Which one of the following measuring instruments measures in newtons?

   ☐ An ammeter

   ☐ A speedometer

   ☐ A voltmeter

   ☐ A forcemeter

3. Convert the following masses from grams (g) to kilograms (kg):

   a. 1000 g = ____________________ kg

   b. 100 000 g = ____________________ kg

   c. 7000 g = ____________________ kg

   d. 500 g = ____________________ kg

4. Convert the following masses from kilograms (kg) to grams (g):

   a. 2 kg = ____________________ g

   b. 50 kg = ____________________ g

   c. 72 kg = ____________________ g

   d. 1.5 kg = ____________________ g

5. What is the weight (in newtons) of the following masses?

   a. 1 kg = ____________________ N

   b. 100 kg = ____________________ N

   c. 25 kg = ____________________ N

   d. 500 g = ____________________ N

Practising my science language

1. Unscramble the letters below to get the name of the English scientist who first explained gravity.

   a s c a I o n w e N t

   The scientist was called ____________ ____________

2. Here is a forcemeter in action.

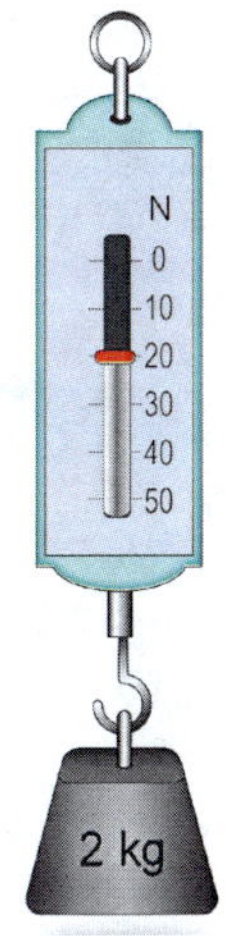

   In your own words, describe how a forcemeter works.

   Include the following words in your answer:

   spring pointer newtons hook

   ____

   ____

   ____

   ____

3. What is the reading on the following forcemeters?

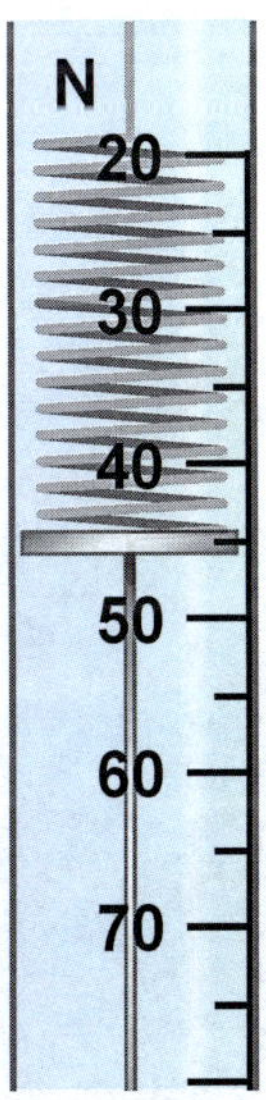

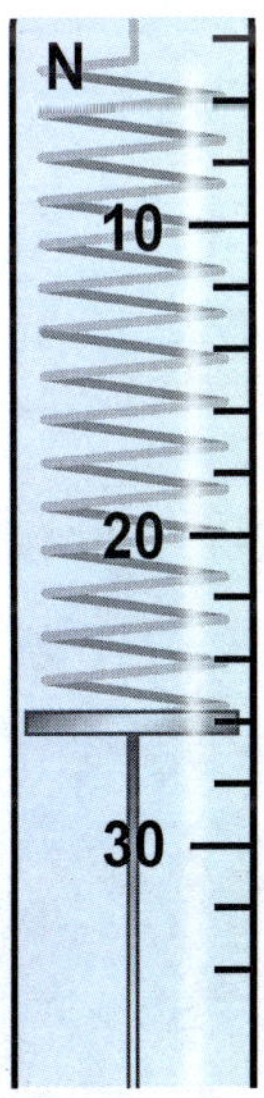

   ____________ ____________

From school to home

Ask an adult at home to help you ...

1. **Talk to an adult about what you know about the difference between the mass and the weight of an object and how to use a forcemeter to measure weight. Explain how to calculate the weight of an object when you know the mass. Practise saying the key words. Use the key words in sentences.**

2. **Now ask someone at home to help you complete the following questions:**

a What did you like about this topic?

____

____

____

b What was hard to understand about this topic?

____

____

____

I understand. I understand a bit. I need more time to understand this.

3 **Look at the checklist below. How are you doing now? Circle one face for each statement.**

- I can explain the difference between the mass and the weight of an object.
- I can use a forcemeter to measure weight.
- I can use the units of force (including weight) and mass.
- I can calculate the weight of an object when I know its mass.

4 **Ask an adult at home to read and sign this.**

I have checked learning on this topic.

We have shared some understanding at home.

Signed: ______________________

Date: ______________

Teacher comment: ______________________________

____

Date: ______________

6.2 Forces and force diagrams

In this second topic in the unit you should be able to name different types of forces and use arrows on diagrams to show the direction of a force.

You should also be able to describe the effects a force can have on an object, as well as what happens when forces are balanced and when they are unbalanced.

Simone is watching TV with her brother, but she is finding it boring. She starts thinking about the work on balanced forces that she did at school today.

Explain what is happening as Simone imagines three different forces acting on her brother.

1. ______________________________

____

2. ______________________________

____

3. ______________________________

____

Explain to someone at home what the cartoon shows.

Check your science!

1. Which two statements about a force are false? Tick two boxes.

A force can:

- ☐ make a stationary object move
- ☐ make an object cool down
- ☐ make an object speed up
- ☐ make an object slow down
- ☐ make an object transparent
- ☐ make a moving object stop
- ☐ make a moving object change direction
- ☐ change the shape of an object.

2. Look at the force diagrams below.

Decide whether the ball would move to the left (←), to the right (→) or not at all (remain stationary).

Tick the correct box for each force diagram.

a. i)

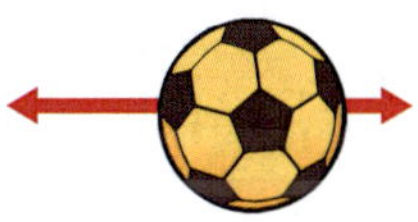

☐ Left ☐ Right ☐ No change

ii)

☐ Left ☐ Right ☐ No change

iii)

☐ Left ☐ Right ☐ No change

iv)

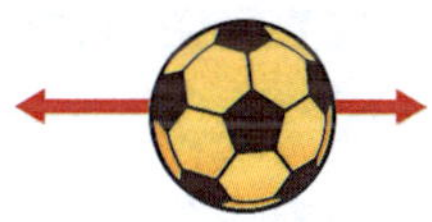

☐ Left ☐ Right ☐ No change

b. Which parts above show an example of balanced forces?

Tick one or more boxes.

☐ part **i)** ☐ part **ii)** ☐ part **iii)** ☐ part **iv)**

c. Draw two force arrows on a tennis ball, in opposite directions, which could make the ball move to the right:

Practising my science language

1. Describe four examples where you apply the following types of forces:

   a. A pulling force: ____________________

   b. A pushing force: ____________________

   c. A squeezing force: ____________________

   d. A twisting force: ____________________

   e. Cross out the incorrect word in bold in the following sentence:

   When each of the forces applied in parts (a) to (d) cause an object to move, we say that the forces are **balanced / unbalanced**.

2. Fill in the blank in each sentence using the word balanced or unbalanced:

   a. An object standing still has ____________ forces acting on it.

   b. An object starts to move when forces become ____________.

   c. ____________ forces will change how quickly an object moves.

3. Read this information carefully.

   A ball has four forces acting on it.

   One force acts vertically upwards. This is the same size as a force acting vertically downwards on the ball. They are the two smallest forces acting on the ball.

   The largest force acts horizontally on the ball, to the right (→).

   The last force is half the size of the largest force and acts horizontally to the left (←).

   a. Draw the force diagram of this ball in the space above.

   b. Describe the movement of the ball in the force diagram.

   ____

From school to home

Ask an adult at home to help you ...

1. **Talk to an adult about what you know about naming different types of forces and using arrows on diagrams to show the direction of a force. Make sure you describe the effects a force can have on an object, and what happens when forces are balanced and when they are unbalanced. Practise saying the key words. Use the key words in sentences.**

2. **Now ask someone at home to help you complete the following questions:**

a What did you like about this topic?

____

____

____

b What was hard to understand about this topic?

____

____

____

I understand. I understand a bit. I need more time to understand this.

3 **Look at the checklist below. How are you doing now? Circle one face for each statement.**

- I can name different types of force.
- I can use arrows to show the direction of a force.
- I can recognise the effects a force can have on an object.
- I can explain what happens when forces are balanced and when they are unbalanced.

4 **Ask an adult at home to read and sign this.**

I have checked learning on this topic.

We have shared some understanding at home.

Signed: ______________________

Date: ______________

Teacher comment: ______________________________

____

Date: ______________

6.3 Friction

In this final topic in the unit you should be able to explain the force of friction, and know that air resistance acts as a type of friction.

You should also be able to investigate how friction affects the movement of objects.

Hana is trying to find out which shape travels fastest through a thick liquid. She makes the different shapes from modelling clay. Then she drops them down a long tube of thick liquid.

This is what happens in her tests.

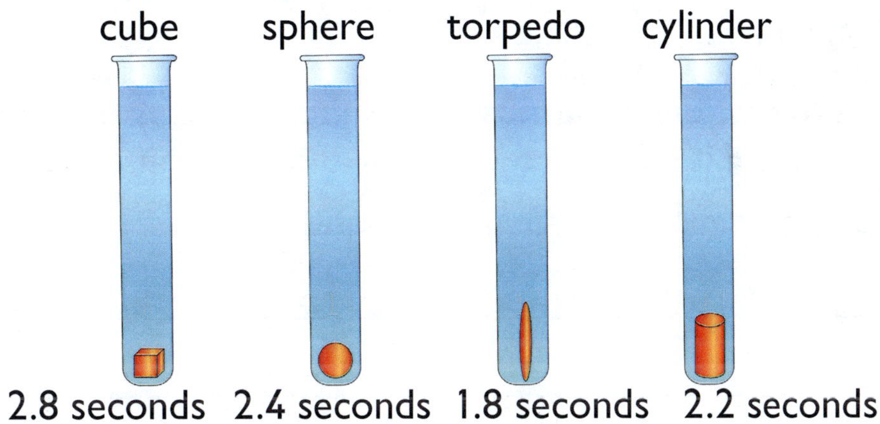

1. Fill in Hana's results in the table below:

Hint

Do not forget to put headings in the top row!

2. Explain what happened in the tests. Include the word "friction" in your answer.

____

____

Discuss and explain this investigation into friction with an adult at home. Say how the investigation was made a fair test.

Check your science!

1. The engine in this car provides a force to the left and the car starts to move left.

   Draw a force arrow to show the friction acting between the wheels of the car and the surface of the road.

2. A group of students are making parachutes out of plastic sheeting, with pieces of cotton tied to the edges and the ends stuck in a ball of modelling clay.

   They decide to test different masses of modelling clay attached to the parachute to see if it affects how quickly the parachute will fall.

   a. What question are the group investigating?

   ____

   ____

   b. Name two factors they should keep the same in each test to make sure the investigation is fair.

   ____

   ____

   c. Make a prediction for this investigation, explaining what you think will happen.

   ____

   ____

   ____

   d. How will the group measure how quickly the parachute falls?

   Include the name of the measuring instrument.

   ____

   ____

Practising my science language

1. What do we call the force of friction that slows down objects as they fall through the air? Fill in the missing letters below.

a _ _ r _ _ _ _ _ _ _ _ _ _

2. Three groups tested two different parachutes, labelling them 1 and 2.

One group used a stop-clock to do the timing, another used a stop-watch and the last group just used the clock on the classroom wall.

Read and record the time taken in seconds for parachutes 1 and 2 to fall to the ground in each group's tests.

a. Group 1 used a stop-clock.

Parachute 1 Time = ________ s   Parachute 2 Time = ________ s

b. Group 2 used a stop-watch.

Parachute 1 Time = ________ s   Parachute 2 Time = ________ s

Practising my science language

c. Group 3 used the classroom clock.

Start time

Finish time

Parachute 1 Time = ________ s

Start time

Finish time

Parachute 2 Time = ________ s

d. Which group used the most accurate measuring instrument?

Tick the correct group.

☐ Group 1 ☐ Group 2 ☐ Group 3

From school to home

Ask an adult at home to help you ...

1. Talk to an adult about what you know about the force of friction, as well as air resistance as a type of friction. Explain how you investigated how friction affects the movement of objects. Practise saying the key words. Use the key words in sentences.

2. Now ask someone at home to help you complete the following questions:

a What did you like about this topic?

____

____

____

b What was hard to understand about this topic?

____

____

____

I understand. I understand a bit. I need more time to understand this.

3 **Look at the checklist below. How are you doing now? Circle one face for each statement.**

- I can explain the force of friction.
- I know that air resistance is a type of friction.
- I can investigate how friction affects the movement of objects.

4 **Ask an adult at home to read and sign this.**

I have checked learning on this topic.

We have shared some understanding at home.

Signed: ______________________

Date: ______________

Teacher comment: ______________________________

____

Date: ______________